Gifts in
JARS

Gifts in JARS

Homemade Cookie Mixes, Soup Mixes, Candles, Lotions, Teas, and More!

Natalie Wise

Skyhorse Publishing

Skyhorse Publishing books may be purchased in bulk at special discounts for sales promotion, corporate gifts, fund-raising, or educational purposes. Special editions can also be created to specifications. For details, contact the Special Sales Department, Skyhorse Publishing, 307 West 36th Street, 11th Floor, New York, NY 10018 or info@skyhorsepublishing.com.

Skyhorse® and Skyhorse Publishing® are registered trademarks of Skyhorse Publishing, Inc.®, a Delaware corporation.

Visit our website at www.skyhorsepublishing.com.

10 9 8 7 6 5 4 3 2 1

Library of Congress Cataloging-in-Publication Data is available on file.

Cover design by Abigail Gehring
Cover photos by Natalie Wise

Print ISBN: 978-1-5107-1974-3
Ebook ISBN: 978-1-5107-1975-0

Printed in the United States of America

CONTENTS

Introduction

I love giving gifts. I love crafting, creating, and offering presents made with my time and creativity. It fills a need deep in my own soul and hopefully fills a space in the heart of the receiver, too. Gifts let us celebrate the big and small accomplishments of life: graduating college, having a baby, or simply . . . Thursday. Thursdays are my favorite.

Creating gifts by hand means investing your life in someone else. You trade your time, which is in essence your life, for something you think will make that someone happy. What a wonderful exchange for happy hearts. I love it.

Gifts are great, but what makes gifts in jars special? First of all, jars are often at hand and easily accessible, making crafting homemade gifts a snap. Secondly, they offer a different take on "wrapping" things by making the presentation part of the gift. The self-contained nature of gifts in jars is exciting and different. Not to mention they're cute, and a ribbon tied around the top makes them even cuter.

I'm excited to share more than fifty ideas for gifts in (and made from) jars, both new and vintage. The jars come in all shapes and sizes, and the gift ideas are for everyone in your life. Let's take a closer look at jars, and then get crafting!

All About Jars

Jars are such a prevalent commodity in our ordinary lives that we often overlook their aesthetics in the name of practicality. They are workhorses, they serve a function, and they serve it well: jars hold things.

Yes, they hold things, from home-canned pantry staples to marbles, pennies, and buttons. There is a sense of nostalgia in a row of jars, solid and sturdy should anything happen to next year's crop or should we need an extra button for mending.

Jars also hold unlimited opportunity for creativity. They can hold things, become things, be passed on or passed around, and be enjoyed again and again. Jars are beautiful as well. Their simplicity belies their beauty, keeping it hidden until we decide to see it.

Why, yes, a jar looks absolutely lovely filled with fresh flowers. How charming she looks with a little necklace of twine and gingham. How punchy on a desk, topped with citrus colors and holding desk supplies. How retro in a child's room, brightly colored and neatly organized.

The abundance of jars in our daily lives makes them ideal for gift giving because they are easy to find when crafting inspiration strikes or we need a last-minute present.

I keep a stash of unique jars on a small shelf under my kitchen sink for just this purpose. I collect spice jars, old candle jars, jars from specialty foods, and antique jars, too.

Jar History

Mason jars, the classic canning jar we use today, was invented in 1858.

The name Mason comes from its inventor, John Landis Mason. Screw-top jars are the most popular for food preservation. Lightning jars, invented by Henry William Putnam, brought the glass-top and wire-bale closure system into use in 1882, and it was popular for a few centuries. Many other companies copied his technique. Antique Lightning brand jars come in various shades of blue, green, and yellow. Mason jars are also called Ball jars, named after the glass manufacturer the Ball Corporation, which was founded in 1880.

Anatomy of a Jar

Mason Jar

Mason Jar

Regular Mouth vs. Wide Mouth: "Regular mouth" jars have a narrower opening with an outer diameter of 2¾ inches. "Wide mouth" jars have a wider opening with an outer diameter of 3⅜ inches. Which you choose depends on use and aesthetics. Some people prefer the more "jar-like" shape of the regular mouth, while others prefer the easier access of a wide mouth jar.

Two-piece lids: Two-piece screw-on lids include a flat top lid with a ring of rubber on the inside to help the seal and a separate band to secure the lid while canning. Antique zinc lids use a rubber ring as the seal inside the lid.

One-piece lids: One-piece lids are not suitable for actual canning but work great for freezer jams and crafts.

Lightning Jar: This jar has a separate glass lid held in place by a two-piece wire bale.

Lightning Jar

Swing-Top Bale Jar: The swing-top jar has become popular recently because it combines the easy-to-open qualities of the lightning jar with the security of a two-piece lid. The bale (two-piece wire closure) is attached to the other side of the jar by a small hinge. These lids may or may not have a rubber seal around the inside to provide an airtight seal.

New Jars

Brand new jars are preferable for any recipes for food or drink use. They are sturdy, won't have any nicks or cracks, and come in every shape and size.

Reusing Jars

Jars from food items are great to reuse for gift jars. Baby food jars are great for small projects, and jam jars are perfectly sized for little hands to hold. Take a stroll down the food aisles and look at all of the different jars available: rounded, straight-sided, and of every size imaginable. Olive jars are tall and narrow, ideal for some projects, and salsa jars are squat, which works best for other projects. Of course, be sure all jars are fully cleaned and sanitized before reusing.

Swing-Top Bale Jar

Antique Jars

Antique canning and pickling jars are no longer suitable for actual canning and pickling, but they make fantastic gift jars. The blue glass jars from Lightning, Hazel Atlas, and Ball are particularly sought-after by collectors for their distinctive hue. Many antique jars are missing their glass lids that were held on by the bale (the two-piece metal hinge), but that won't matter for many gift jars. Also look for the milk-glass-lined zinc lids that were used as a unique topper on vintage jars that didn't have a bale. No need to use the rubber rings unless you want an airtight seal.

Tips and Tricks

- New jars and most reused jars can go through the dishwasher to easily sanitize them before using them to hold gifts.
- If you don't have a dishwasher, simply boil jars for five minutes to sanitize the glass.
- To get stubborn, sticky labels off reused jars, simply let soak in warm water with a bit of dish soap. The labels should slide right off, leaving no residue.
- Wide, shallow jars are particularly hard to come by. Snatch these up when you find them.
- Never used chipped glass or glass jars with cracks. Glass with any damage becomes very unstable and can easily break.
- A bottle brush is handy for cleaning many jars that you can't fit your hand into or that the dishwasher doesn't get clean.
- If the bale on the jar is rusty, use a bit of steel wool to gently release the rust.
- Soak scummy jars in white vinegar for at least half an hour before cleaning with a soft plastic scrub brush. Don't use steel wool on the jar itself as it will scratch the glass.

Jar Math

Use this handy conversion chart to figure out how big your jars are and how much they'll hold. The best way to tell is to fill the jar with water, then pour that water into a large measuring cup.

¼ cup = 2 ounces
½ cup = 4 ounces
¾ cup = 6 ounces
1 cup = 8 ounces = ½ pint
1¼ cups = 10 ounces
1½ cups = 12 ounces
1¾ cups = 16 ounces = 1 pint
2 cups = 18 ounces
3 cups = 24 ounces
4 cups = 32 ounces = 1 quart
5 cups = 40 ounces
6 cups = 48 ounces
7 cups = 56 ounces
8 cups = 64 ounces = ½ gallon

Tools to Make Jar Crafts Easier

- Wide-mouth canning funnel
- Regular-mouth funnels of various sizes
- Chopsticks to move items in tall jars
- Tweezers to move items in small jars
- Measuring cups and measuring spoons
- Small brush to clean off jars after adding flour, cocoa, glitter, etc.

Tools for Decorating Jars

- Hot glue gun
- Chalk paint
- Chalkboard paint
- Spray paint
- Decoupage medium such as Mod Podge
- Glue dots
- Fabric
- Ribbon and twine
- Hang tags
- Paint markers
- Glass paint
- Glitter
- Washi tape

Kitchen

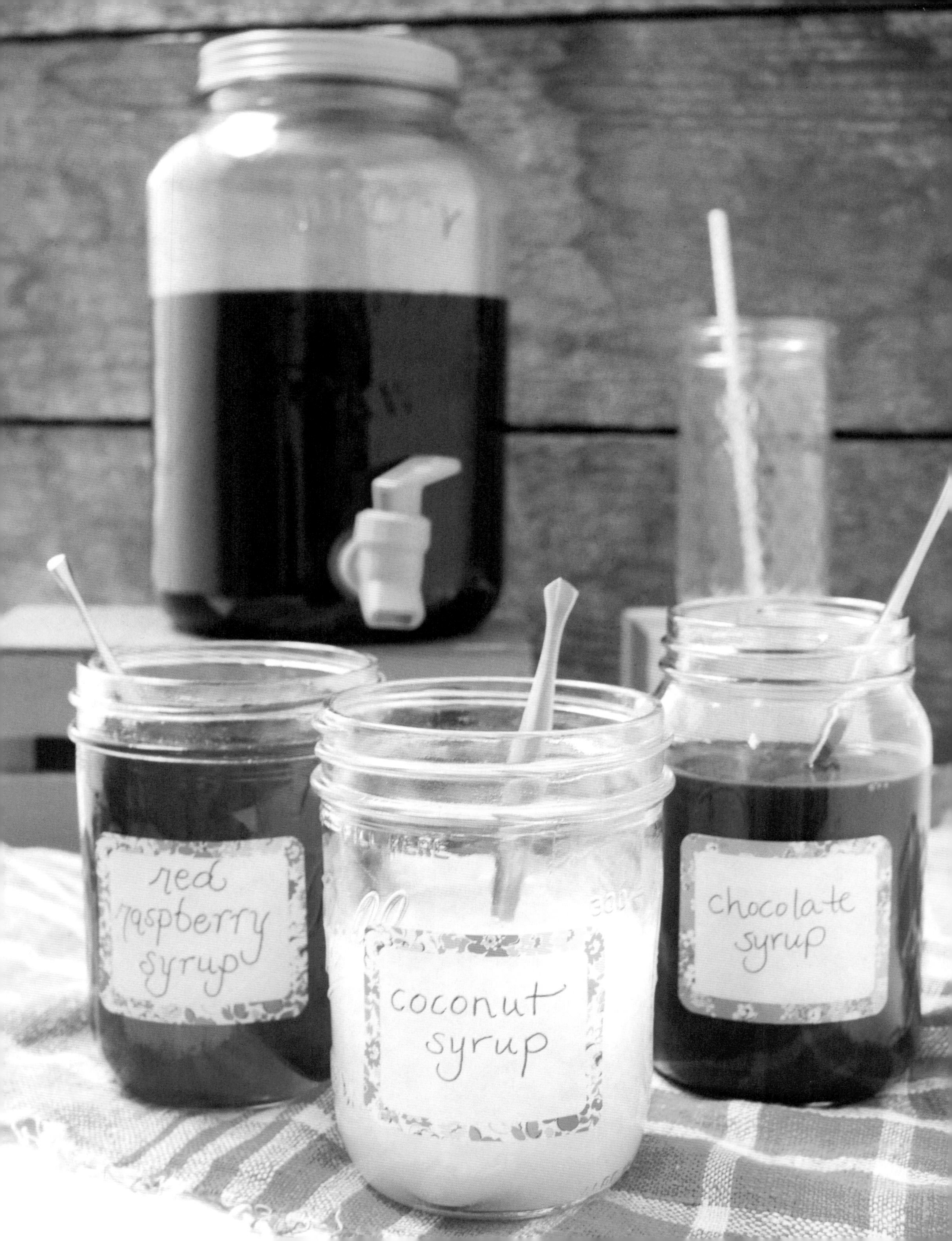
red raspberry syrup
coconut syrup
chocolate syrup

Coffee Syrups

. . . .

Coffee syrups are a cinch to make at home and the colors are so pretty in glass jars. Coffee syrups make great hostess gifts, especially if you include a package of coffee. Or set them out at your own party and make a coffee bar, then give away tiny jars as favors. The syrups work in both cold and hot coffee, which is part of their appeal. Don't forget to mix and match. Chocolate-raspberry? Tastes like dessert. Raspberry-coconut? A tropical vacation.

Each recipe makes: approx. 2 cups

Jar size in photo: 1 pint

Chocolate Syrup

Ingredients
Jar of choice
Tight-fitting lid
1½ cups water
1 cup cocoa powder
1 cup sugar
¼ tsp. salt

Whisk all ingredients together in a small saucepan over medium heat. Whisk constantly until mixture comes to a boil. Boil for 2–3 minutes, until smooth, and remove from heat. Funnel into jar. Will keep for several weeks in the refrigerator.

Coconut Syrup

Ingredients
Jar of choice
Tight-fitting lid
1½ cups water
1 tablespoon sugar
¾ cup sweetened flaked coconut

Combine all ingredients in a small saucepan and stir to combine. Heat over medium-high heat, stirring frequently, until mixture comes to a boil. Reduce heat to a simmer and simmer for 5 minutes. Strain through a fine mesh strainer. Funnel into jars. Will keep for several weeks in the refrigerator.

Raspberry Syrup

Ingredients
Jar of choice
Tight-fitting lid
1½ cups sugar
1½ cups water
¾ cup fresh raspberries

Combine all ingredients in small saucepan over medium heat and stir until the sugar is dissolved and the mixture comes to a gentle boil. Mash the raspberries using a metal potato masher or the back of a spoon. Turn heat to medium-low and let simmer for 10–15 minutes, stirring frequently so it doesn't burn. Strain through a fine mesh strainer to remove seeds and pulp. Funnel into your jars and let cool. Will keep for several weeks in the refrigerator.

Tag Instructions: Stir 2–4 tablespoons into your coffee beverage of choice. Keep syrup in refrigerator.

Best-Ever Barbecue Rub

This barbecue rub is sure to become an oft-requested gift, particularly by the grill masters in your life. This recipe makes the perfect amount to fill two small shaker jars, the ideal size for keeping by the grill or stove. Look for jars with the holes in a star shape instead of "S" and "P" for salt and pepper. The stars allow a generous flow of rub. There should be enough left over for your own dinner tonight . . . try it on chicken, ribs, or pork.

Makes: Just over 1 cup

Jar size in photo: 4 ounces

Ingredients
2 jars of choice
Tight-fitting lids
½ cup paprika
⅓ cup brown sugar
3 tablespoons chili powder
1 tablespoon onion powder
1 tablespoon pepper
1 tablespoon salt
2 teaspoons garlic powder
1 teaspoon cayenne pepper

Mix well in a small bowl, then funnel into your storage jars. If you live in a humid place, store shakers in a resealable bag to keep moisture out.

Iced Tea Jar

· ·

This is such a fun hostess gift for any summer barbecue. But these teas are also just as enjoyable hot and can be given any time of year. The debate between sweetened and unsweetened tea is long-standing, so I suggest filling the bottom of the jar with individual sugar packets to let everyone choose their level of sweetness. Look for the tea and dried flowers in the bulk section of your local grocery or health food store.

Makes: 1 gift jar

Jar size in photo: ½ gallon

Ingredients

Jar of choice
Tight-fitting lid
1 cup orange pekoe tea
1 cup dried hibiscus flowers
Cheesecloth
Baker's twine
Assortment of citrus fruit: oranges, lemons, limes
Straws
Individual packets of sugar
Colorful rubber spatula

> OTHER TEA COMBINATION IDEAS FOR HOT OR ICED TEA:
>
> **Lemon Mint:** 1 cup lemon balm, 1 cup spearmint leaves (add lemons and limes to jar)
>
> **Earl Gray-Lavender:** 1 cup earl gray tea, ¼ cup dried lavender (add lemons and a small jar of honey)

Cut 4 squares of the cheesecloth about 6 inches square. In the center of each square, place ¼ cup of orange pekoe tea and ¼ cup hibiscus flowers. Gather the corners and tie with twine. Set aside. Place the sugar packets on the bottom of the jar and layer the fruit on top. Gather the straws and place them down the height of the jar on one side. Gently place the 4 tea bags you've created on top. Close the lid and tie a cute spatula around the mouth of the jar.

Tag Instructions: To cold brew: Slice the fruit and add back to the jar. Place 1 tea bag in the jar and fill with cold water. Stir. Close the lid and let sit in the refrigerator overnight. Serve over ice with sugar, if desired, and straws. Can also be brewed and served hot.

Hot Fudge Topping

My friend who owns an ice cream parlor declared this hot fudge topping "Spectacular!" and asked if she could trade me a jar for an ice cream sundae. Then she asked me to make it and sell it in her shop. Success! This recipe makes two jars, one for keeping and one for giving (or two for giving if you're feeling generous).

Makes: approx. 4 cups

Jar size in photo: 12 ounces

Ingredients

2 jars of choice
Tight-fitting lids
¾ cup heavy cream
½ cup light corn syrup
½ cup packed brown sugar
½ cup cocoa powder
½ teaspoon salt
8 ounces dark chocolate, chopped
2 tablespoons unsalted butter
1 tablespoon vanilla extract

In a saucepan over medium heat, combine the heavy cream, corn syrup, brown sugar, cocoa powder, salt, chocolate, and butter. Bring to a boil, then reduce the heat to a simmer and stir constantly for 5 minutes. Remove from heat and stir in the vanilla extract. Pour into jars and let cool. Will keep refrigerated for several weeks, but I doubt it will last that long.

Tag Instructions: Store in refrigerator. Before eating: warm desired amount in microwave or double boiler.

Blueberry Refrigerator Jam

This is an excellent jam for beginners because it doesn't require processing in a hot water bath. Since the recipe makes a small batch and is kept in the refrigerator, there's no need for an actual seal that will last for years. You and your friends will definitely gobble this up long before it goes bad. You will want to boil the clean jars for 5 minutes, though, for safety's sake. A jar lifter (a specialized canning tool), will be enormously helpful for getting the jars out of the hot water, but tongs used carefully will suffice.

Makes: 1½ pints

Jar size in photo: 12 ounces

Ingredients

8–10 cups (4 pints) blueberries, picked over
2¼ cups sugar
1 Tablespoon lemon zest
1 Tablespoon lemon juice

In a large saucepan, place your two pint jars, lids, and rings, and fill with water. Set on a back burner. In a medium saucepan, combine the blueberries and sugar. Turn on the heat to medium and use a metal potato masher or the back of a spoon to mash the blueberries well. Cook until gently boiling. Stir constantly or the jam will burn. Be careful because happy bubbling jam is hot and will splatter. Stir for at least 30–45 minutes, until thick and the spoon faces resistance as you try to stir. When you get to the last 10 minutes, bring the large saucepan with the jars and lids to a boil. When your jam is ready, remove it from heat. Carefully remove the jars one at a time and place on a heatproof surface. Remember not to touch the jars as they are hot. Ladle the jam into the jars. Let cool on the counter for several hours, then cover and refrigerate. Will keep for several weeks in refrigerator.

Tag Instructions: Store in refrigerator.

Monster Brownie Mix

. . . .

These brownies are perfect to keep on hand when a craving hits. There's hardly anything to making them, and in minutes you'll have a gooey, peanut-buttery, chocolatey, nutty treat warm from the oven. These are a take-off on the classic Monster cookie, which has every tasty treat packed in it. It's a lucky friend who receives this pretty—and yummy—brownie mix.

Makes: 1 mix for a 9x9-inch pan of brownies

Jar size in photo: 1 quart

Ingredients

1 jar of choice
Tight-fitting lid
¾ cup flour
½ tsp. salt
½ cup cocoa powder
½ cup flour
¾ cup packed brown sugar
⅔ cup white sugar
½ cup colored chocolate candies
½ cup peanut butter baking chips
½ cup nuts
2 tablespoons flour

Layer the ingredients in the jar in the order listed. At the end, toss the nuts with the additional 2 tablespoons of flour so they won't sink to the bottom of the brownies when mixed. Close tightly and decorate jar with ribbons and the initials of the recipient, if desired.

Tag Instructions: Pour the contents of the jar into a large bowl and stir. Add 1 teaspoon vanilla, 2/3 cup vegetable oil, and 3 eggs. Mix well. Pour into a greased 9x9 pan and bake at 350 degrees for 25–30 minutes.

Cut-Out Sugar Cookie Mix

It's tough to find a sugar cookie mix that works well for rolling out shapes. This one fits the bill and makes a perfect holiday gift. The resulting cookies are only slightly sweet, a pleasant base for plenty of icing and decorations. Attaching a cookie cutter to the jar is particularly fun. For kids, add dinosaurs or flowers. For adults, unique shapes such as the Mason jar pictured are a great addition to their cookie cutter collection.

Makes: 1 mix for about 1½–2 dozen cookies, depending on size

Jar size in photo: 24 ounces

Ingredients

3 cups flour

1 teaspoon baking powder

½ teaspoon salt

1½ cups sugar

Mix the ingredients together in a large bowl and funnel into the jar.

Tag Instructions: Cream 1 cup (2 sticks) butter with 1 egg and 1 tablespoon vanilla until smooth. Slowly add in the cookie mix until it comes together. Refrigerate dough at least 15 minutes. Roll and cut with cookie cutters. Bake at 350 degrees for 8–10 minutes, until just golden around the edges.

Soup Mixes

· ·

Soup jars make such a good holiday gift for anyone in your life. Not only are they pretty, they're sure to be appreciated on a cold winter's night when soup sounds just right, but something quick and easy is needed. Buy your ingredients in the bulk section and use a funnel to make creating these gifts even simpler.

Lentil-Curry Soup Mix

Makes: 1 jar, 4–6 servings

Jar size in photo: 1 pint

Ingredients
1 cup green lentils
2 tablespoons curry powder
1 teaspoon onion powder
1 teaspoon garlic powder
1 teaspoon celery salt
2 tablespoons dried basil
1 cup red lentils
3 slices freeze-dried apples

Layer the ingredients in the order given, placing the freeze-dried apple slices on top just under the lid.

Tag Instructions: Empty mix into soup pot and add 3 jars full (6 cups) of water. Simmer for 30 minutes or until lentils are tender.

Chicken Soup Mix

Makes: 1 jar, serves 8–10

Jar size in photo: 1 quart

Ingredients
½ cup dried veggie mix (in the bulk or spice section)
¼ cup chicken bouillon granules
1 teaspoon dried dill
1 teaspoon garlic powder
1 teaspoon onion powder
About 2 cups dried noodles (may need more, depending on shape, to fill jar)

Layer the seasonings on the bottom of the jar, and then fill with noodles.

Tag Instructions: Bring 8–10 cups of water to a boil. Add contents of jar. Simmer for 20–30 minutes, or until noodles are tender. Add cooked chicken if desired.

5-Bean Soup Mix

Makes: 1 jar, serves 10–12

Jar size in photo: 1 quart

Ingredients
1 teaspoon onion powder
1 teaspoon garlic powder
1 teaspoon salt
1 teaspoon pepper
¾ cup dried red beans
¾ cup dried great northern beans
¾ cup dried split peas
¾ cup lentils (any color)
¾ cup dried black beans

Tag Instructions: Add soup mix, 8 cups of water, and 1 (15-ounce) can of crushed tomatoes to a large pot. Simmer for at least 1½ hours, until beans are tender.

Hot Chocolate Mix

Hot chocolate mix is a coveted item around the holidays, especially a homemade, luxurious one that's rich in cocoa powder and chocolate. Using milk powder in the mixture allows the recipient to just add water to create this creamy cocoa. Top the mixture with plenty of marshmallows, and perhaps even tie a small bottle of festive sprinkles around the lid. A vintage Santa ornament will work, too, to complete the gift and presentation.

Makes: 1 jar, 12 servings

Jar size in photo: 1 quart

Ingredients
1¼ cups unsweetened cocoa powder
1¼ cups sugar
1 cup powdered milk
½ teaspoon salt
½ cup miniature chocolate chips
1 cup miniature marshmallows

Combine the cocoa, sugar, powdered milk, and salt. Mix well and funnel into jar. Layer the miniature chocolate chips and miniature marshmallows on top.

Tag Instructions: Mix 1/3 cup hot chocolate mix into 1 cup boiling water. Stir well.

Spiced Granola with Nuts, Coconut, and Chocolate

* *

Crunchy, hearty granola with yogurt and fruit is my go-to breakfast every morning. This flavorful granola also makes a great snack by the handful. Use any type of coconut you have on hand . . . thick strips, angel flaked, or unsweetened flakes. Any nuts you happen to have will work here; I used cashews for this batch, but almonds, pecans, and walnuts also work well. Regular chocolate chips will work, too, but the miniature ones are just the right size for the oats and ground nuts and are a fun surprise. Don't add them too soon after taking the granola out of the oven, or they'll all melt. This recipe perfectly fills a 1/2-gallon jar or 2 quarts, with just enough left over for your breakfast!

Makes: 8 cups

Jar size in photo: ½ gallon

Ingredients

6 cups old-fashioned oats
¼ cup brown sugar
½ cup vegetable oil
⅓ cup honey
2 teaspoons vanilla
2 teaspoons cinnamon
1 teaspoon ground ginger
1 cup shredded coconut (sweetened or unsweetened)
1 cup chopped nuts (your choice)
½ cup mini chocolate chips

Preheat oven to 350 degrees and line a baking sheet or two (depending on their size) with parchment paper. Place the oats in a large bowl. Add the brown sugar and mix well. In a separate small bowl, mix the vegetable oil, honey, vanilla, cinnamon, and ginger well. Pour over the oat mixture and mix well to coat all of the oats. Stir in the coconut and nuts, reserving the chocolate chips. Pour onto the lined baking sheet and spread into an even layer. Bake for a total of about 30 minutes, stirring every 5 and rotating the sheet halfway through the baking time. Let cool. When mostly cool, stir in the chocolate chips. Stays fresh in an airtight container for several weeks.

Bath and Body

Vanilla Citrus Sugar Hand Scrub

Makes: 2 cups

Jar size in photo: 8 ounces

Ingredients

1 cup sugar

Zest of 1 medium orange

1 teaspoon honey

¼ cup light olive oil

1 teaspoon vanilla

Mix ingredients until very thoroughly mixed. Pack into jars. Keep the lids on tightly as the scrub tends to dry out and may need a good stir now and then. Will keep for several weeks.

Tag Instructions: Rub vigorously on hands to exfoliate. Rinse well.

Coffee Lover's Body Scrub

Coffee has long been known for its cellulite-reducing properties when applied topically. I can't promise any magic cures, but at the least this body scrub will wake you up in the morning with its pleasant aroma. This makes a great gift for any coffee-lover in your life. Other coffee scrubs can be drain-clogging, but this one doesn't have enough coffee to cause a problem, so don't worry.

Makes: approx. 2 cups

Jar size in photo: 8 ounces

Ingredients

Jars of choice
Tight-fitting lids
2 cups sugar
1 cup light oil, such as olive, almond, or apricot
3 tablespoons finely ground coffee

Mix all ingredients together well. Pack into jars.

Tag Instructions: Massage all over body in shower. Let sit for a few minutes before rinsing well.

Mojito Lip and Face Scrub

. . . .

This face and lip scrub is a lovely addition to any spa night or daily routine. The scent is invigorating and refreshing. Your skin and lips will be chap-free and smooth as can be. There is no oil in this recipe, so it won't clog your pores or separate. Just use a teaspoon or so in the palm of your hand with a little bit of water.

Makes: approx. 1½ cups

Jar size in photo: 4 ounces

Ingredients
Jars of choice
Tight-fitting lids
1½ cups sugar
2 teaspoons salt
2 teaspoons lime zest
2 teaspoons finely chopped fresh mint

Whir the sugar and salt in a food processor until they are very fine. Add the lime zest and mint. Pack into jars.

Tag Instructions: Place a small amount of scrub in your palm, add a bit of water, and massage onto lips and face to exfoliate.

Pretty Pink Bath Soak

This gorgeous gift is sure to be on display in the recipient's bathroom. Try to find a sculptural jar for this beautiful pink bath soak. This is an antique sugar jar, but anything with a bit of fanciness will suffice. Rose oil is wonderful for your skin, and ylang ylang is calming and soothing. Feel free to experiment with essential oils here, or leave them out altogether if you prefer a scent-free product. While this makes a perfectly lovely gift on its own, I also like to tuck a small jar into the Sleep Sweet kit on page 41.

Makes: 1 jar, 8 ounces

Jar size in photo: 6 ounces

Ingredients
8 ounces pink Himalayan salt, coarse ground
8 drops rose absolute essential oil
8 drops ylang ylang essential oil

Mix the salt and essential oils together well. Funnel into jar.

Tag Instructions: Add ¼ cup to a hot bath for relaxation and rejuvenation.

Lemon-Lavender Body Lotion

This luscious lavender body lotion is the perfect gift for anyone who lives in a cold climate. The shea butter locks in moisture and skin drinks up the coconut oil. This will keep solid in cold climates, but if you live in a warm area, store in the refrigerator to prevent separating and melting. If it melts, just stir it together again and let it solidify in the refrigerator. I love lemon-lavender for a refreshing yet stress-relieving scent, but feel free to try other essential oils as well.

Makes: approx. 18 ounces

Jar size in photo: 4 ounces

Ingredients
1 cup solidified coconut oil
¼ cup shea butter
8 drops lemon or lemongrass essential oil
8 drops lavender essential oil

Combine all ingredients together in an electric mixer fitted with a paddle. Whip until light and well mixed, at least 5 minutes. Transfer to jars. Keep refrigerated if necessary.

Manicure Kit

Manicure kits are a go-to for women of all ages who love to be pampered. From bright, glittery polishes for the young ones to sophisticated neutrals for adult friends, a manicure-at-home kit will refresh any lady in your life. Choose items that color coordinate, and consider adding some or all of the extra luxuries listed below to make this a full spa kit. Don't forget the basics so she has everything she needs for a great manicure: nail clippers, cotton balls, nail polish remover, a nail file, and a cuticle stick. Single-use nail polish remover pads will fit in here perfectly; find them in the nail polish aisle.

Makes: 1 manicure kit jar

Jar size in photo: 12 ounces

Ingredients
Jar of choice
Cotton balls
Hair ties
Nail polishes
Top coat
Nail embellishments
Nail polish remover
Nail file
Nail brush
Nail clippers
Cuticle stick
Face mask
Lip balm
Lotion

Layer cotton balls in the bottom of the jar to serve as a base. Add a few hair ties on the bottom for color if desired. Prop the items in a pleasing way, showcasing colors and shapes, with a few items peeking out over the top of the jar. Tie with ribbon or a hair tie.

Sweet Sleep Kit

This kit is perfect for the overworked and overtired. Be that a college student, a new mom, or a best friend, it seems everyone is desperate for a good night's sleep. Give someone sweet dreams with this zzzzz-inducing jar. I love to tie a sleep mask or spa mask around the jar for extra encouragement of sweet dreams.

Makes: 1 sweet sleep kit jar

Jar size in photo: 32 ounces

Ingredients
Jar of choice
¼ cup dried lavender blossoms
Stress relief lotion or aromatherapy spray
Small jar of bath salts
One bath tea sachet (see page 47)
2–4 herbal tea bags
One shower burst or bath bomb (see page 45)
Sleep mask, optional

Place the lavender blossoms in the bottom of the jar. Arrange the rest of the items in the jar. Tie a sleep mask around the jar, if desired.

Rosewater

. . . .

Rosewater is expensive to buy but takes minutes to make at home. It's the perfect gift for someone who has everything. Use it as a linen spray, body spray, aromatherapy spray, or facial mist. The rose essence is calming and healing for skin and mind. Look for bulk organic dried rose petals in your local natural health food store. The recipe couldn't be simpler, and the aroma while you're making it? Heavenly. Keep this refrigerated so it stays fresh and refreshing.

Makes: approx. 1½ cups

Jar size in photo: 12 ounces

Ingredients
Jar of choice
Airtight lid
1 cup fresh or dried organic rose petals
2 cups distilled water

Place the rose petals in a heat-proof bowl and set aside. Bring the 2 cups distilled water to a boil. Remove from heat, pour over rose petals, and immediately cover the bowl with a lid to lock in the steam. Let sit undisturbed for 30 minutes. Strain the rose water into jars. Let cool. Keep refrigerated.

Tag Instructions: Use this pure rose water as an aromatherapy mist, body spray, linen spray, or face mist. Keep refrigerated.

Sea Breeze Bath Bombs

. . . .

These light blue bath bombs are sure to be savored by the lucky recipient. They fizz and settle into a delightfully restorative bath soak, filled with the fragrance of a sea breeze. Vetiver and lemon essential oils are known for being uplifting, and together their sweet fragrance is intoxicating. They are also both excellent for detoxifying. Depending on the size of your container, this recipe makes approximately 4–6 bath bombs.

Makes: approx. 4 5–ounce bath bombs

Jar size in photo: 1 quart

Ingredients

Jar of choice
½ cup Epsom salts
1 cup baking soda
½ cup citric acid
½ cup cornstarch
¾–1 teaspoon water
12 drops vetiver essential oil
12 drops lemon essential oil
A small dot of gel blue food coloring (or a few drops of liquid)
Mold of choice (or muffin tin with cupcake liners)

Place the Epsom salts in a food processor and blend until fine-grained. Place in a large bowl. Add the baking soda, citric acid, and cornstarch and mix well. In another small bowl, mix together the water, essential oils, and food coloring. Add to the dry ingredients and mix well. The mixture will feel like sand, but if you press it together it should hold. Add water, a tiny amount at a time, until it sticks together when pressed firmly. Pack into both halves of your mold, then press the mold together to seal. You can also firmly pack into a muffin tin with cupcake liners. Let dry overnight, then unmold and package in jars.

Tag Instructions: Add 1 sea breeze bath bomb to your hot bath. Relax and be transported to a sandy beach.

Refreshing Bath Tea

This bath tea will bring refreshment to your body and mind to wake you up after a long day. The spearmint is cooling, the lemon balm has a calming effect, and the roses relax muscles. The scent alone will perk you up. The mixture looks pretty enough to eat, so be sure to keep this out of reach of children since it has essential oils in it. One scoop, about ¼ cup, is perfect per bath.

Makes: 3 cups

Jar size in photo: 24 ounces

Ingredients
Jar of choice
1 cup dried spearmint
½ cup dried lemon balm
½ cup dried red rose petals
½ cup dried pink rosebuds
½ cup dried lavender
6 drops lemongrass essential oil

Mix ingredients together and pour into jar.

Tag Instructions: Refreshing Tub Tea: add ¼ cup to your hot bath for a relaxing and uplifting soak.

For the Home

Candles with Wood Wicks

. . . .

These glamorous candles are perfect gifts for just about anyone in your life, male or female. They are great hostess gifts and also work for neighbors, teachers, friends, and family. No one will believe you made these, so don't tell them how easy they are. Spray paint elevates the humble jar to knock-out status for a gift that's sure to impress. Make as many as you'd like, figuring on 2 ½–3 cups of soy wax flakes per jar.

Makes: 3 4-oz. jar candles

Jar size in photo: 4 ounces

Supplies
3 small jars, lids optional
Gold metallic spray paint
Clear spray paint overcoat, if desired
9–10 cups soy wax flakes
3 wood candle wicks with clips
4 ounces essential oil of your choice

Spray paint the jars of your choice with gold metallic spray paint. Finish with a clear overcoat if you wish. If you don't overcoat them, the jars will "age" a bit, which adds a shabby-chic glamour that I happen to like. Prepare your finished and dried jars by placing them in a row close to your candle-making station. Fit a wood wick into the wick clip and place in each jar. Place the soy wax flakes inside a metal, heatproof pitcher with a pouring spout. Place that pitcher inside a small pot and fill the pot with water until it reaches 2 inches up the side of the pitcher. Bring the water to a boil and let the soy wax flakes melt completely (they will do so quickly). Remove from heat. Carefully, using an oven mitt, remove the pitcher from the boiling water and stir in the essential oils. Then carefully pour the wax into each jar, filling almost to the top. Straighten the wicks when you've poured all the candles. Let set at least 24 hours before moving or burning.

Crafts in a Jar

Anyone crafty or with a talent for creative pursuits is sure to love a jar filled with more supplies for their favorite, or a new, medium. Just about any craft or art can be condensed into jar form. Here, I've compiled mosaic tiling supplies, knitting supplies, watercolor supplies, and ink drawing supplies in various jars. Look for small, unique items related to their craft, such as this tiny 2x3 inch canvas I found at the art store.

Makes: 4 jars (one for each artistic medium)

Jar sizes in photo: 1 quart, 1 pint, 12 ounces, and 8 ounces

Supplies

For the Mosaic Tile Jar:
Jar of choice, lid optional
Enough mosaic tiles to fill your jar
A small tube of mosaic glue or E600 glue
A package of mosaic grout to include

For the Knitting Jar:
Jar of choice, lid optional
Various knitting needles
Small balls or skeins of yarn (look on the endcaps at the craft store)
A pattern or two

For the Watercolor Jar:
Jar of choice, lid optional
12 small tubes watercolor paint, or enough to fill your jar
2 small paintbrushes
A small canvas

For the Ink Drawing Jar:
Jar of choice, lid optional
A small bottle of ink
A small mister
A pack of Fantastix Coloring tools

Arrange items artfully in each jar.

Happiness Jar

The happiness jar is one of my favorite things to give friends for birthdays or if they are going through tough times. The idea of a jar filled with good things at the end of a year is uplifting indeed. Since the jar will be mostly empty to begin with, I love to put a few flowers in there to brighten things up as well. Collect ticket stubs, business cards, lucky pennies, and more. Add a stack of blank notes and some pens so your friend can write down all of the little, wonderful memories from the year. Emptying it out and going through it all at the end of the year is sure to bring smiles.

Makes: 1 jar

Jar size in photo: 12 ounces

Supplies
Jar of your choice
A few small mementos or trinkets
Fresh flowers, preferably in water tubes
Ribbon
At least 25 blank business cards
Colorful pens

If the flowers are in water tubes, great! Now you can simply slip them into the jar with the mementos, add a few notes of encouragement for your friend on a handful of the blank business cards, tie the others up with ribbon, and tuck it all, with the pens, in the jar.

Tag Instructions: Remind yourself of the happy little things in life. Add a note or memento that makes you happy every day!

Scented Oil Diffuser with Reeds

. . . .

Scented oil diffusers are great because they don't use any electricity and continually produce aromatherapy. They also happen to have a cool modern aesthetic that I love. Look for unique jars with narrow openings for this project. The low jar pictured here is a vintage oil lamp. Tall jars from olives also work well. Feel free to switch up the essential oils, as always, but aim for combinations that offer refreshment or relaxation.

Makes: 1 oil diffuser

Jar sizes in photo: 12 ounces and 16 ounces

Supplies

Jar of choice with narrow neck
Any light oil, such as almond or apricot oil
Orange essential oil
Geranium essential oil
6–12 wooden reeds or kebab skewers

Fill the jar with the carrier oil until it is about ⅓ full. Then add the essential oils. I used 24 drops total per cup of oil, but adjust according to the amount of oil in your jars. Top with lid for transport and tie the reeds around the jar. Refresh scent by flipping the reeds upside down every few days or so.

Tag Instructions: Place reeds in oil for a light aromatherapy scent. Flip reeds every few days to refresh scent.

Soap or Lotion Dispenser

This is such a fun, beautiful, and useful gift, particularly as a housewarming present. Mercury glass is making a comeback from its old-fashioned roots and shines beautifully. Spray paint and household vinegar make the job of transforming a plain jar into gorgeous mercury glass easy. Of course, smooth-sided jars work best for this technique. Reuse pretty soap dispenser tops, or you can purchase one at your local craft or home goods store. Fill it with a luxuriously scented hand soap or lotion.

Makes: 1 soap/lotion dispenser jar

Jar size in photo: 1 pint

Supplies
1 smooth-sided pint jar
1 2-piece jar lid
Awl or other sharp instrument to make hole in lid
Hammer
Pliers
E600 glue
Mirror-effect spray paint (such as Krylon's "Looking Glass")
White vinegar
Water

Fill a spray bottle with ¼ cup vinegar and ¼ cup water and shake to combine. Spray the jar with the mixture, then immediately spray with the mirror-effect spray paint. Continue this technique until the jar is covered and dry. Repeat with a second coat if you like a deeper color. While that dries, prepare the lid. Use an awl and a hammer to pierce a hole in the center of the flat part of the lid. Use the plier to open the hole wide enough for the soap dispenser bottom to fit through. Put a thin ring of E600 glue around the edge of the soap dispenser bottom where it will be flush against the lid, and thread it through the hole, pressing into place until dry. Then, simply fill the jar with soap, add the lid, spin the ring into place, and voila!

Drink Cup with Straws

· ·

These jars are just utterly fun. Make them in bunches; everyone will want one. I collect fun straws during the year for various holidays and occasions and stockpile them for summer drinks. Pretty much any jar will work to make a drink cup. Don't forget to place the hole for the straw near the edge to make it easier to drink. The rubber grommets can be found at your local hardware store with the plumbing supplies. Bring a straw with you to make sure you get the correct diameter. I also purchased larger rubber grommets for use with smoothie and milkshake straws.

Makes: 1 drinking jar

Jar sizes in photo: 12 ounces, 1 pint, and 20 ounces

Supplies
Jar of your choice
1 or 2-piece lid for jar of choice
Awl or other sharp instrument to make hole in lid
Hammer
Rubber grommets
Pliers
Fun straws

Place the awl where you'd like your straw hole to go, and hit it with the hammer to make a hole. Then use the pliers to expand the hole in a circle to just smaller than the diameter of the grommet. Fit the grommet into the hole, using the rubber sides to cover any sharp edges created by expanding the hole. Screw the lid on with the band and insert straw.

Flower Arrangement in "Hob Nob" Vase

Hob nob milk glass is a favorite of vintage collectors everywhere. The glossy white, combined with the little "nobs" makes for a simple but lovely jar. You can recreate the look on any jar, no scouring of thrift stores required. A little hot glue and spray paint will do the job just as well. The jar will be treasured long after the flowers are gone. My friend who owns a flower shop said, "What a lovely vintage vase!" when I brought this in to have her make a gorgeous bouquet for it. Your friend will be just as delighted.

Makes: 1 jar vase

Jar size in photo: 54 ounces

Supplies

Large jar of your choice
Hot glue gun
Hot glue (you'll need plenty)
Glossy white spray paint
A gorgeous flower bouquet

Using a very hot hot glue gun, make dots of glue all around the jar at various intervals. These do not need to be in straight lines or symmetrical. Try to keep the dots as round as possible (getting your glue gun as hot as possible helps). When all of the glue dots are dry, carefully use scissors to snip off any glue strings. Then spray paint the jar with glossy white spray paint. When dry, fill with gorgeous flowers.

use
it up
. . . .
wear
it out
make
it work
. . . .
or do WITHOUT.

Sewing/Mending Kit

Mending seems to be a lost art, but those who do mend today do so in unique ways, with colorful patches and seams, embroidery, and all sorts of creativity. This jar has all of the accessories needed for the budding seamstress or anyone interested in learning the lost art of saving your favorite clothes by mending them. The wooden implement is a darning "egg;" place it inside a sock or under the area where the garment needs darning or mending to fill it out and allow you to mend correctly.

Makes: 1 sewing jar

Jar size in photo: ½ pint

Supplies
Jar of choice
Clothespins
Hem tape
Rick-rack or other fanciful trim
Spools of thread in various colors
Mending wool
Mini sewing scissors
Mini clothespins
Wash-out clothing pencil
Small pin cushion
Hand sewing needles in small needle book
Sewing pins in small box
Darning egg

Fill the bottom of the jar with clothespins. Add the trims and small box of pins. Fill the jar with the rest of the items.

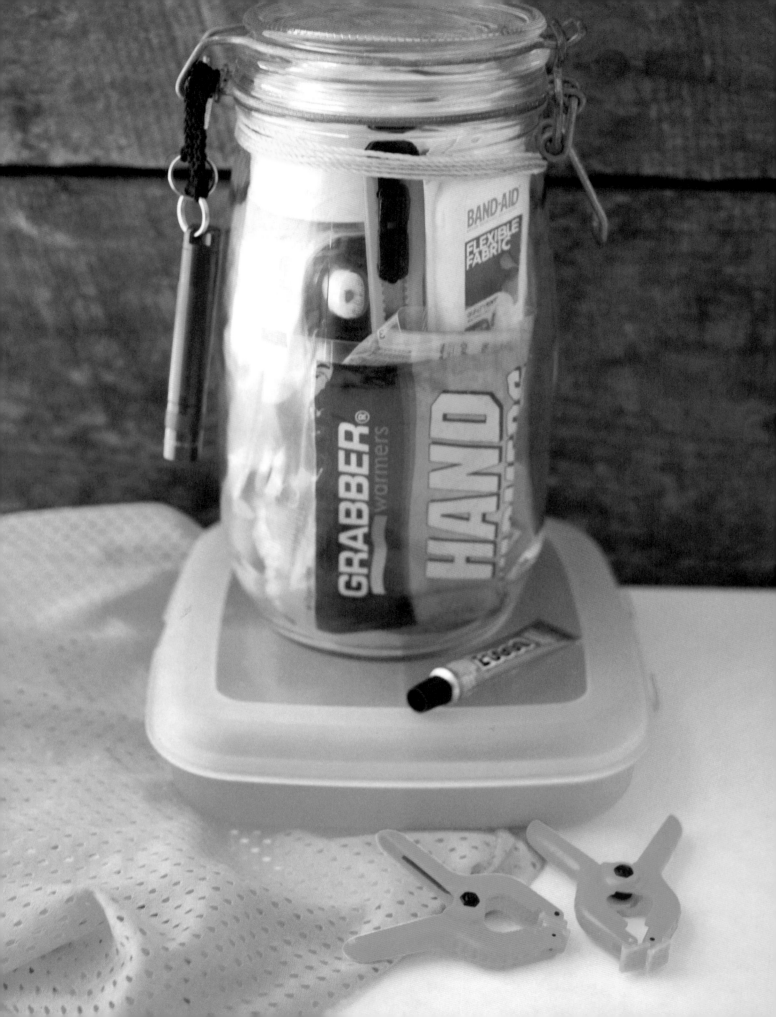

Emergency Kit

This is a great gift for anyone, but especially for those who live alone, travel frequently, or are just moving into a new home. It is useful to have everything necessary for small and large emergencies (power outages, minor injuries) at hand and in one place. This is only a partial list of items that would be useful in the jar. Stashing a little cash in this jar isn't a bad idea either; sometimes emergencies require a coffee or ice cream run.

Makes: 1 emergency jar

Jar size in photo: 54 ounces

Supplies
Jar of choice
Tight-fitting lid
Small flashlight
Emergency blanket
Gauze pads
Roll of gauze
Elastic bandage
Bandages in various sizes
Waterproof tape
Waterproof matches
High-protein snack, such as a protein bar or small cup of peanut butter
Mini toothbrush
Hand warmers
Box cutter
Strong string or paracord
Mini clamps
E600 glue
Small notebook
Pen
List for emergency contact info and medicines/allergies
Mini flashlight and replacement battery

Fill the jar with the items and close tightly. I like to keep the flashlight on the outside, so it can be easily accessed in an emergency.

Tag Instructions: Open in case of emergency.

Party and Kids

Big Bubbles with Wands

Giant lawn bubbles are sure to amaze kids and make you the best aunt, friend, or babysitter around. Make homemade wands, too. The kids were obsessed with the heart wand I made, but the giant bubble maker was fought over, too. Make a whole bunch so sharing is easier. The color of the bubble mixture will depend on the dish soap you use. Keep in mind that some natural dish soaps don't contain the same foaming agents and may not produce ideal bubbles.

Makes: ½ gallon

Jar size in photo: ½ gallon

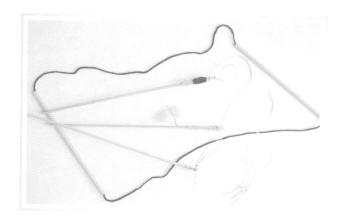

Supplies
Jar of choice
Airtight lid
12-inch dowels
18 gauge stainless steel wire
Wire cutters
Yarn, ribbon, tassels, etc., to decorate wands
2 plastic straws
1 yard of string or yarn
8 cups of distilled water
1⅓ cups dish soap
1½ tablespoons glycerin

To make wands: Wrap a few inches of the wire around the end of the dowel, then create a design such as a heart or spiraling circles, before bringing the wire back around and wrapping a few more times on top of the initial wraps. Snip off sharp edges. Wrap the wire end with twine or ribbon, adding tassels or decorations if desired. For the bigger bubble wand, feed the string through both straws and tie the ends of the string together. Feed the knot through one of the straws so it disappears. To use, hold the straws close together and dip them and the string in the bubble solution. Lift and spread the straws apart, then blow into the middle to create a large bubble.

To make bubble mix: Slowly and carefully mix all ingredients together in the jar. Try not to create any air bubbles. To use, pour into a large, shallow dish, such as a baking pan or laundry tub. Will work right away, but for bigger bubbles, let mixture sit overnight.

Playdough

Homemade playdough comes together in a snap and is fun to make. The colors turn out just as bright as store-bought varieties, and when kept airtight it lasts just as long. What child wouldn't love a jar full of rainbow playdough and a jar full of miniature cookie cutters to play with? Using gel food coloring will get you the brightest colors, and don't be afraid to raid the cake decorating department of your crafts store. They have an array of gel food coloring options, including neon colors.

Makes: 2 playdough jars, or about 2½ cups of playdough

Jar size in photo: 12 ounces

Supplies
2 jars of your choice
Tight-fitting lids
1 cup flour
½ cup salt
1 cup water
2 tablespoons vegetable oil
2 teaspoons cream of tartar
Gel food coloring in colors of your choice

Combine ingredients in a medium, heavy-bottom saucepan. Heat over medium heat, stirring frequently, until it begins to combine. Then, stir constantly until the mixture comes together away from the pan and has the consistency of playdough. Let cool until cool enough to handle but still warm. Divide into pieces and make a small depression in the middle of each piece. Place a large dab of gel food coloring in the middle of each piece. Cover the food coloring with dough, then knead it together until the color is thoroughly absorbed and even. Keep covered in an airtight container.

Snowglobe Scenes

. . . .

These snowglobes are pretty perched in any corner or on a desk or bookshelf, coffee table, or mantle. Customize the scenes any way you like. Here, I went for a vintage shabby-chic style that included pink-dyed, vintage-style bottle brush trees dipped in snow and frolicking gold deer. Tiny musical instruments were left in the snow after festivities, and glitter abounds to make things sparkle. Look for tiny ornaments, presents, pinecones, mail boxes, trees, animals, and baskets. Tweezers are very helpful for arranging the small items.

Makes: 1 snowglobe jar

Jar size in photo: 8 ounces

Ingredients
Jar of choice
Artificial snow
Glitter
Miniature bottle-brush trees
Miniature ornaments
Miniature woodland animals
Miniature instruments

Place a 1" layer of artificial snow in the bottom of the jar, and top with glitter. Arrange your elements in a pleasing way.

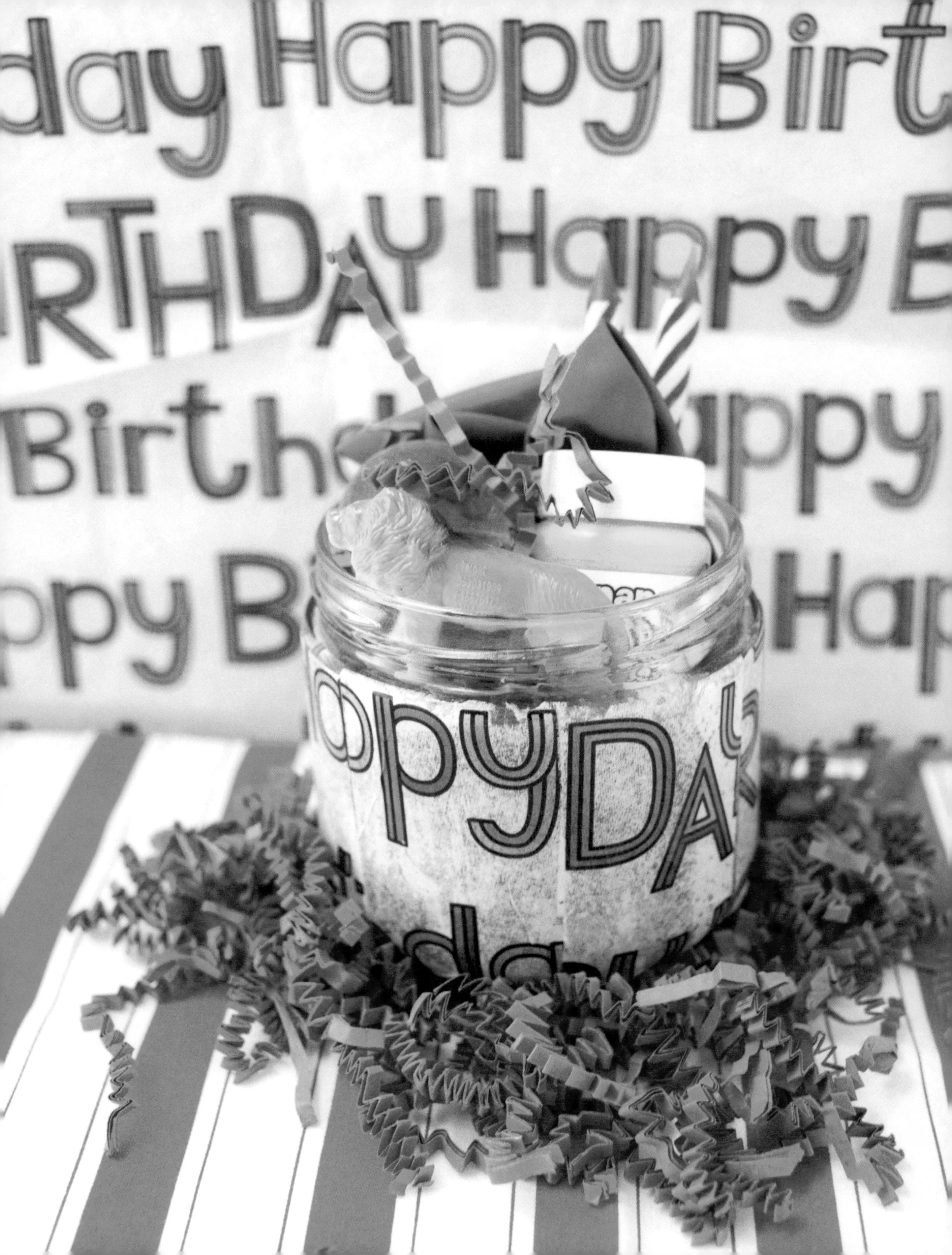

day Happy Birt

"Piñata" Prize Jar

....

This piñata jar was inspired by a few traditions that I love. My friend's kids get to choose a treat from the "kindness box" at school when they are good sharers, extra quiet, or otherwise polite and kind. And then there are surprise balls, where layers of tissue paper are wrapped around small treasures to create a ball for children to unwrap on special occasions. Of course, every kid (and kid at heart) also loves a piñata, so this prize jar is perfect for kids of all ages. When you've put all of the goodies in the jar, add more party paper shred so none of the surprises are visible.

Makes: 1 piñata/prize jar

Jar size in photo: 8 ounces

Supplies
Jar of choice
Decoupage medium, such as Mod Podge
1-inch foam brush
Tissue paper in a fun pattern or design
Small bowl for Mod Podge
Scissors
Waxed paper
Red paper party shred
Balloons
Small treats, such as figurines, small bottles of bubbles, crayons, marbles, bouncy balls

Lay out the waxed paper on your work surface. Cut the waxed paper into strips about 4 inches long and 2 inches wide, to cover the length of the jar. Dip your foam brush in decoupage medium, coat the jar where the tissue paper strip will go, lay down the strip, then thoroughly coat the strip again with decoupage medium. Continue around the jar, overlapping strips if you need to. Let dry upside down overnight. Fill the jar with party shred, balloons, and treats before covering with more party shred.

Road Trip Kit for Kids or Adults

· ·

Road trips are fun. They can also be boring for long stretches if you don't have the right supplies on hand. I love using the chalkboard spray paint on these jars. It makes use of the jar itself as another surface for games and coloring. Straight-sided jars without words or designs will work best for this. Adults need their own sort of kit to handle the road trip, filled with essentials to ease the open road, so I've included options below for an adult alternative.

Makes: 1 road trip jar

Jar size in photo: 24 ounces

Supplies
Jar of choice
Chalkboard spray paint
Chalk
Small games, toys and treats such as miniature games, stickers and a sticker book, koosh ball, mini rubber chicken, mini Slinky toy, mini Etch-a-Sketch toy, crayons, etc.

ADULT VARIATION:

The adult version can include packets of pain reliever and upset stomach reliever, tissues, trail mix, lip balm, chewing gum, a personal fan, and earplugs.

Spray paint the jar with chalkboard spray paint. Let dry completely. Then label the jar with chalk. Fill the jar with games and toys to keep the child entertained.

Party in a Jar

The party in a jar is one of my classic and most favorite jar projects. I love to send these to friends who are far away, or leave them for friends when I won't be able to attend their party. They can be themed to any age or occasion. I did a girly pink-and-candy themed party jar and a luau jar, but use your imagination. Simply find party favors and fun little gifts and gadgets to add to the fun of the day, and pack it all into a jar for instant happiness.

Makes: 1 pink-themed jar and 1 luau-themed jar

Jar sizes in photo: 18 ounces and ½ gallon

Supplies

For Pink Jar:
Jar of choice, lid optional
Pink and yellow balloons
Pink paper party shred
Pink, green, yellow, and white pom-poms
1 cup licorice All-Sorts candy
2 colored candy sticks
4–5 festive drink picks
1 pink rock candy stick

For Luau Jar:
Jar of choice, lid optional
1–2 fake flower leis
Yellow paper party shred
Large umbrella drink picks
Large fruit honeycomb drink picks
1–2 1-ounce bottles of rum
Tropical themed cocktail napkins

Layer the ingredients in each jar festively and present with gusto.

Kids Fun Gifts/Storage

A dime-store bag of jumbo jacks, marbles, or plastic army men is much more enticing in a jar with a chartreuse giraffe, don't you think? These not only organize (older kids will love to sort their building blocks by color) but add color and whimsy to any playroom. Be sure to let the animals dry thoroughly on their perches before proceeding with spray paint. Since the animals are generally brightly colored, a base coat of white spray paint makes all trace of their previous colors disappear.

Makes: 3 storage jars

Jar size in photo: 8 ounces

Supplies
Jars of choice
One-piece lids
Plastic animal figurines
E600 glue
White spray paint
Glossy spray paint in the color of your choice
Small toys or figurines to fill jars

Add a dab of E600 glue to each foot of the animal and apply it firmly to the center of the jar lid. Repeat for each jar. When the glue is completely dry, give the animals and lids a base coat of white spray paint. Once dry, coat a few times with the colored spray paint, turning as necessary after each coat to cover thoroughly. Fill jars with toys.

Mini Aquarium

This is such a fun gift for older children or anyone who could use a colorful friend to keep them company. All of the supplies can easily be found at the pet store, sans the jar, which you'll need to find at your craft store. A 32-ounce jar or larger works well for a beta fish or guppie. You can also opt for a plastic fish and tint the water blue for younger kids. Of course, don't put a lid on the jar once it has an actual fish inside.

Makes: 1 aquarium jar

Jar size in photo: 32 ounces

Supplies
Jar of choice
1 pound aquarium gravel
10 flat-backed blue glass gems
1 aquarium plant
Distilled water
Water conditioner
Small fish
Fish net
Fish food

Layer the gravel in the bottom of the jar and nestle the bottom of the aquarium plant into the gravel. Top with the glass gems, covering the rest of the bottom of the plant so it is secure. Add distilled water and water conditioner according to package directions. Let water sit for 24 hours. Then, using the small net, transfer the fish to the new jar. Of course, it's best to present this pet with the fish net and food for its new owner.

Glow in the Dark Fairy/Milky Way Jar

This glow-in-the-dark jar is almost a science project, it's so cool. It's perfect for taking to sleepovers or drive-in movies. The glow will last as long as a glow stick normally would—at least a few hours. The glitter creates an extra fanciful element. The finer the glitter, the better the effect. Try different colors of glow sticks, or line up several different-colored jars for a rainbow look. When making these as a gift for other people, I like to fill the jars with uncut glow sticks and a tube of glitter, so the recipients can make these fun lanterns themselves (instead of giving an already-glowing jar)! While adults should cut open the glow sticks, don't worry; the contents of glow sticks are non-toxic, so if some spills or gets on your skin, simply rinse it off.

Makes: 1 light-up fairy jar

Jar size in photo: 1 quart

Supplies
Jar of choice
1 large glow stick
1 tablespoon glitter

Break open the glow stick carefully using scissors. Add the oil (if there is any) and the fluorescent fluid to the jar. Add the glitter to the jar. Close tightly and shake. Will glow for several hours.

Cupcake Decorating Kit

Cupcakes are a go-to for children's parties, grown-up parties, and even weddings, so who wouldn't love a kit with everything necessary to create showstopper cupcakes? Budding bakers and professionals alike will enjoy this sweet gift. A theme works well for this kit, so use a coordinating color or pattern for all of the goodies. You'll need a wide-mouth jar for this project, so the cupcake wrappers can fit in easily.

Makes: 1 cupcake decorating kit

Jar size in photo: 32 ounces

Ingredients
Wide-mouth jar of choice
Paper party filler
3–4 kinds of cupcake wrappers, at least 12 of each
1–2 kinds of mini cupcake wrappers, at least 8 of each
Birthday candles
Sprinkles in small containers
Small cake decorating writing gels
Small cupcake flags on toothpicks
Cupcake toppers, such as paper flowers, edible sugar pearls, icing decorations, etc.
Ribbon for decorating

Begin by covering the bottom of the jar with party filler. Stack the cupcake wrappers in alternating colors, with the mini cupcake wrappers on top, flipped upside down so they make a small perch for the other items. Carefully lower the stack into the jar, making sure it is centered. Then, place birthday candles around the bottom back half of the jar, pressing them tightly against the glass behind the cupcake wrappers. Prop the writing gels on top of the candles on one half of the back, and prop the cupcake flags on the other half. Fill the center with the small jar of sprinkles and the cupcake toppers. Tie ribbon around the jar top and affix tag, if desired.

Tag Instructions: Cupcake Pretties

Sleepover/Camp Survival Kit

Sleepovers and sleep-away camp are growing-up rituals. These kits are specially designed to make a sleepover evening or week unforgettable. Some of the items are practical, such as an anti-itch stick for bug bites, others designed to help them make friends, such as mini playing cards. A few extra dollars is always welcome for snacks at the camp canteen or a late night ice cream treat.

Makes: 1 sleepover/camp survival kit

Jar size in photo: 8 ounces

Supplies
Jar of choice
Band aids
Candy bar
Mini flashlight
MadLibs game
Glow-in-the-dark tattoos
Anti-itch stick
Miniature playing cards
Journal
Pen
Five-dollar bill

Place all items in your jar.

For and From the Garden

Tillandsia

FROM

J. L. DUNNELL,

DEALER IN

Flour, Grain, Feed and Hay,

NORTHFIELD,

Bags.

cks.

Air Plant Garden

Air plants (officially called Tillandsia) are amazing little things . . . they don't need soil for their roots to survive. An every-other-day gentle mist keeps them happy. They come in all sorts of shapes and sizes, and create such a fun display. Since they will happily survive without much sunshine, they are perfect for an office desk. Nestle them into rocks and sand for a cool ecosystem.

Makes: 1 air plant jar

Jar size in photo: 8 ounces

Supplies
Low jar with a wide mouth
Sand
Small rocks
2–3 air plants (I used T. ionantha fuego, T. ionantha rubra, and T. butzii)
Fine mister

Place the sand in the bottom of the jar. Arrange the rocks on top. Add the air plants, nestling them in lightly. Mist with water.

Tag Instructions: Air plants love to be misted with water every other day.

Chef's Herbs

. . . .

This darling little herb garden is perfect for the kitchen window sill or front porch. Feel free to arrange the jars in any way you like, and different finishes and shapes of jars keep things interesting. This chalk-paint finish is one of my favorites for a cottage-style look. And, of course, fill them with any variety of herbs you'd like.

Makes: 1 herb garden with 3 jars

Jar sizes in photo: 1 pint, 24 ounces and 18 ounces

Supplies
3 jars of choice
3 small herb plants
Potting soil
Water
Gardening tray

Fill the jars with potting soil, making a large depression in the center for the plant. Place the plant in the depression and fill in with potting soil. Press down lightly and give each plant a thorough watering. Present in a garden tray to complete the look.

Herb Infused Oils

. . . .

Herb infused oils are ideal for the gourmet chef on your gift list. Or the consummate host. Or the one who just loves food. Basically, herb infused olive oil is a great gift for anyone. If you choose to keep the herbs in the oils for a pretty presentation, they will make the oil cloudy and will not last as long. Strain them out if you prefer. Store these lovely oils away from heat and sunlight to preserve their integrity. You'll want to use a light olive oil here instead of extra-virgin, which would compete with the delicate herb flavors.

Makes: 3 jars

Jar size in photo: 4 ounces

Supplies
Three jars of choice
Airtight lids
1½ cups of light olive oil
2–3 fresh or dried bay leaves
2 tablespoons fresh or dried parsley
2–3 stalks fresh rosemary

Place one spice in each jar. Funnel ½ cup of olive oil over the top of each jar. Close tightly. Let sit overnight for flavors to mingle. Strain out the herbs if you desire. Will keep for several weeks if stored airtight.

Sow Shappy Reap Rhappy

Seed Bombs

. . . .

Seed bombs are a term for balls of dirt mixed with seeds thrown into hard-to-reach areas to disperse seeds. These little jars are the same idea . . . throw them anywhere you want a touch of color and a few wildflowers. Look for flowers that grow naturally in a meadow-like environment as they'll do best in nooks and crannies, along walls, in ditches, etc. Any place you need to beautify. These are great fun for a budding gardener . . . the mix of seeds will be wonderful to see sprout.

Makes: 3 seed bomb jars

Jar size in photo: 4 ounces

Supplies
3 jars of choice
Potting soil
3–4 different kinds of seeds that work well in the same growing conditions

Fill the jars with potting soil. Mix the seeds together in a small bowl and place a small amount (depending on the size of the seeds) to each jar. Shake well.

Tag Instructions: Throw this soil into a garden spot that needs some added beauty, and see what grows!

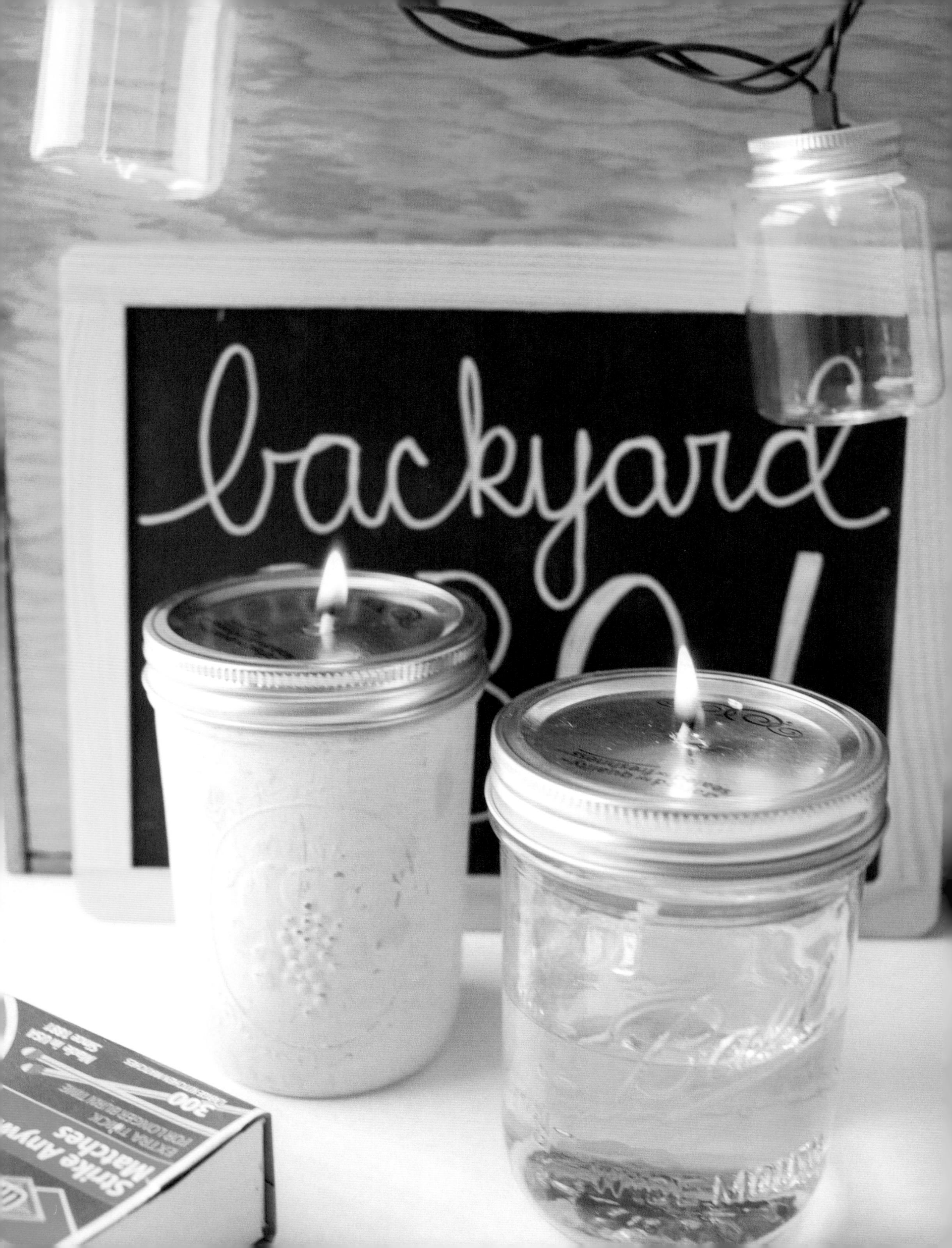
backyard

Citronella Oil Lamp

Citronella oil lamps make any summer outdoor activity more enjoyable. The citronella oil repels mosquitos and the comforting firelight is less obtrusive than a fire pit. I like to use the clean-burning clear citronella oil instead of a blue or yellow liquid most often found in stores because I prefer not having color. But you could also mix and match citronella oil colors for a fun alternative. Be sure to use proper wicking or only 100 percent cotton rope for your wick.

Makes: 1 oil lamp jar

Jar size in photo: 1 pint

Supplies

Jar of choice
Lid
Citronella oil for torches and lamps (not the essential oil)
8 inches of wicking or 100% cotton rope
Awl or other sharp instrument to make hole in lid
Hammer
Pliers

Place the awl in the center of the lid and tap with hammer to create a hole. Use the pliers to make the hole wide enough for the wicking, but not so wide the wicking falls back into the oil. Feed wicking through the jar and leave about 1" sticking out of the top of the jar, with the rest coiled loosely in the jar. Fill ⅓ of the way with citronella oil. Screw lid on tightly. Let the wick soak up oil for at least 20 minutes before burning.

Fairy Garden Kit

Creating little homes for fairies is a pastime that delights all ages. This kit is perfect to tuck into an existing fairy garden, or as the starting point for a new one. I love to use a colored jar for this project. Fairies love sparkly things, so be sure to include lots of gems, mother-of-pearl shells, glitter, and other embellishments. The height of the gem sticks invites fairies to land, and the small swing (partially shown below) is the perfect resting place. My little friend Ellie tells me that fairies sometimes leave presents, too, which is quite exciting.

Makes: 1 fairy garden kit

Jar size in photo: 8 ounces

Ingredients
Jar of choice
Enough potting soil to fill your jar
Various fairy-friendly fillers: shiny wire spheres, gemstones such as amethyst or quartz, shells, etc.
Glitter in the color of your choice

Mix the potting soil and a few shakes of glitter well. Fill the bottom of your jar. Place the embellishments, making full use of the space in the jar, and pushing a few items farther down into the soil so they can be seen from the outside of the jar. Sprinkle extra glitter over all. Place outside in the garden bed, in a flower pot, or any place you desire.

Tag Instructions: Tuck this darling little fairy jar amidst your favorite plants in the garden for good wishes and fairy dreams.

Bug House

. . . .

My friend's two boys, ages 4 and 6, went crazy for these bug houses. They quickly filled them with fresh leaves and grass before going off in search of critters to rehome. Three water striders came home in jars (with added water), and a few other critters. Creating various lids allows critters of different sizes to be captured and able to breathe without getting loose. Use cheesecloth tied on some, and vintage metal flower frogs hinged on with copper wire on others.

Makes: 1 bug house

Jar sizes in photo: 1 quart, 4 ounces, and 8 ounces

Supplies
Jar of choice
Lid of choice: flower frog, gauze, wire-topped lid, or lid with holes poked in it
Drift wood, sticks, leaves, and stones

Place a few pieces of driftwood, sticks, leaves, or stones in the bottom of the jar. If you're attaching a flower frog to the jar, wind copper wire through and around the spokes of the flower frog on one side securely. Then wrap the wire around the jar twice and back through the spokes of the flower frog on the same side. It should hinge nicely now. For the gauze lids, simply tie a square of gauze over the jar. Use to hold bugs for short periods of time while you investigate them.

Zen Garden for Desk

. . . .

This contemplative garden design invites thought. The simple elements and the small rake to play with in the sand remind one to climb into possibility, shift things around, and keep things simple—all things we need to be reminded of during a busy workday. Look for the small bench, rake, and/or a ladder in the miniatures section of the craft store. I also added the gem stone fluorite, known for helping with meditation.

Makes: 1 zen desk garden jar

Jar size in photo: 6 ounces

Supplies
Jar with a wide opening
Sand
Smooth stones
Gemstone such as fluorite
Simple garden miniatures, such as a bench, rake, pail, or ladder

Place the sand in the bottom of the jar. Arrange the items in a pleasing way, just barely placing them in the sand.

Sand and Shells Memory Collector

I love to give this symbolic gift for beach weddings; it's just perfect! Many bridal couples choose to pour two small jars of sand into one large jar as a symbol of their coming together in matrimony. See if you can get ahold of the actual sand they use in the ceremony for an extra special touch. If not, start with one layer of sand, and remind them to add to it when they go on their honeymoon, trips together, and start new phases of life by adding a new layer of sand and a shell or two.

Makes: 1 sand and shells memory collector jar

Jar size in photo: 32 ounces

Supplies

Jar of choice

Photo of the couple

Decoupage medium, such as Mod Podge

Foam brush

Votive candle

3 colors of sand, at least 1 cup of each to get a nice layer

Seashells

Start by decoupaging the photo onto the inside back of the jar. Coat the jar well with decoupage medium where you will be positioning the photo, place it into position, and cover it with another coat. Let dry thoroughly. Then layer the colored sands. Press a few seashells into the sand and place the votive in the middle.

Tag Instructions: Add a layer of sand or a seashell for each spectacular place you visit and new phase in life.

Bird Feeder

This is such a fun gift for any bird watcher or lover. I like to add a coordinating half-gallon jar filled with extra bird seed to make the gift extra special. The small chicken feeders can be found at your local farm supply store and are perfectly made to screw onto a quart jar. These jars are sturdy, but if you have especially large or fierce animals that like to invade your bird feeders, you may want to keep it on a flat surface, such as a railing or table.

Makes: 1 bird feeder jar

Jar size in photo: 1 quart

Supplies
Quart jar
Small chicken feeder
E600 glue
Strong rope
Bird food

Beginning at one jar seam at the top of the jar, just under the rim and threads, secure one end of the rope with E600 glue. Then follow the jar seam, gluing the rope down on the seam as you go. Leave a loop for a handle at the top and then continue gluing down the other seam until you reach the rim on the other side. Cut off and secure the end with glue. Let dry thoroughly. Fill the jar with bird food, keeping it right side up, and screw the chicken feeder onto the jar. Quickly flip. Enjoy.

Garden Marker Rocks

I love these little rocks in small herb garden beds. They're a delightful way to mark herbs and they look pretty, too. I like to mark a few with standard garden herbs such as mint, rosemary, sage, and basil. Then add a bunch of blank stones for the recipient's own garden varieties. Include a waterproof paint pen. An old garden implement is also a welcome addition to this jar.

Makes: 1 jar of garden marker rocks

Jar size in photo: 1 pint

Supplies
Jar of choice

Moss

Smooth black river rocks (look for these in the wreath-making section)

Waterproof paint pen

Vintage garden tool

Place a layer of moss in the bottom of the jar. Fill the jar ¾ full with plain rocks. Write the names of a few common plants or herbs on a few rocks and let them dry completely. Fill the jar with these rocks. Tuck the paint pen and garden tool in the rocks.

Succulents Open Terrarium

Terrariums are all the rage, but a closed terrarium is a delicate ecosystem that takes time and expertise to perfect. These succulent open terrariums have all of the appeal with little of the maintenance. They love a good soaking once they dry out, about once every week or two. You'll also want a good moisture-wicking additive to mix with the soil so the roots don't get too moist. A half-and-half ratio with the soil is ideal. For the jar pictured here, I used wavy jade (crassula arborescens undulatifolia), sedum dasyphyllum, and the "Aurora Borealis plant" (kalanchoe fedtschenkoi Aurora Borealis).

Makes: 1 open terrarium jar

Jar size in photo: 24 ounces

Supplies

Wide-mouth jar of choice
2–3 succulent plants
Potting soil
Perlite, coarse sand, or other moisture-wicking soil additive
One special rock for accent, optional

Mix half potting soil and half wicking additive in a bucket. Fill the jar with the mixture, packing loosely. Gently make depressions on the top and settle the succulents in, patting the mixture around their roots. Nestle the stone in amongst them. Soak with a good watering.

Index